Book Farm

12·12

Lost Cities

by Natalie Lunis

Consultant: Paul F. Johnston, PhD
Washington, D.C.

BEARPORT
PUBLISHING

New York, New York

Credits

Cover and Title Page, © Geo Martinez/Photoxpress and Attilla Huszti/Shutterstock; 4–5, Kim Jones; 6, © Jim Sugar/Corbis; 7, © Jack Fields/Corbis; 8, © Nicola Filardi/ Flickr/Getty Images; 9, © Cubo Images/SuperStock; 10, © The Francis Frith Collection/SuperStock; 11, © Harry Page/The Daily Mirror/Newscom; 12, © David Gray/Reuters/Newscom; 13, © David Gray/Reuters/Newscom; 14, © DEA/M.BORCHI/De Agostini Picture Library/Getty Images; 15, © British Museum/AFP/Getty Images/ Newscom; 16, © Hein von Horsten/Images of Africa Photobank/Alamy; 17, © Claus Brandt/age fotostock/SuperStock; 18, © The Asahi Shimbun/Getty Images; 19, © Sankei/Getty Images; 20, © Scott Peterson/Liaison/Getty Images; 21, © Sergei Supinsky/AFP/Getty Images; 22, © Cypherone; 23, © age fotostock/SuperStock; 24, © Cubo Images/SuperStock; 25, © Warner Brothers/Courtesy Everett Collection; 26, © Peter Connolly/akg-images/Newscom; 27, © Linda Bucklin/Shutterstock; 31, © Nikonaft/Shutterstock.

Publisher: Kenn Goin
Editorial Director: Adam Siegel
Creative Director: Spencer Brinker
Design: Dawn Beard Creative
Cover Design: Dawn Beard Creative and Kim Jones
Photo Researcher: Picture Perfect Professionals, LLC

Library of Congress Cataloging-in-Publication Data

Lunis, Natalie.
 Lost cities / by Natalie Lunis ; consultant, Paul F. Johnston.
     p. cm. — (Scary places)
 Includes bibliographical references and index.
 ISBN 978-1-61772-567-8 (library binding) — ISBN 1-61772-567-6 (library binding)
 1. Extinct cities—Juvenile literature. 2. Ghost towns—Juvenile literature. I. Johnston, Paul F. II. Title.
 CC176.L86 2013
 909—dc23

                                 2012014238

For more information, write to Bearport Publishing Company, Inc., 45 West 21st Street, Suite 3B, New York, New York 10010. Printed in the United States of America.

10 9 8 7 6 5 4 3 2 1

Contents

Lost Cities

Normally, cities are busy, lively places. People work, play, buy and sell **goods**, raise families, and travel back and forth within them. How, then, can an entire city become lost?

Some cities disappear when they are destroyed by a disaster, such as an earthquake, a volcanic eruption, or a flood. Others empty out when the **industry** that gave them their start shuts down. Still others are lost for reasons that are largely unknown.

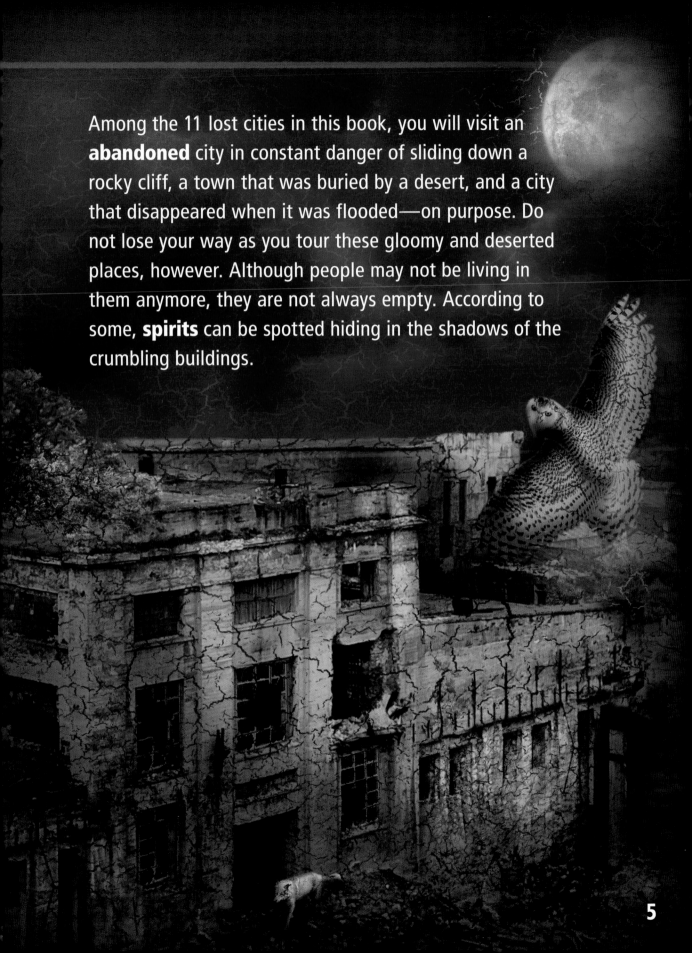

Among the 11 lost cities in this book, you will visit an **abandoned** city in constant danger of sliding down a rocky cliff, a town that was buried by a desert, and a city that disappeared when it was flooded—on purpose. Do not lose your way as you tour these gloomy and deserted places, however. Although people may not be living in them anymore, they are not always empty. According to some, **spirits** can be spotted hiding in the shadows of the crumbling buildings.

Mysterious Islands

Nan Madol, Micronesia

In the middle of the vast Pacific Ocean lies a group of tiny human-made islands surrounded by high walls. Huge, heavy stones were used to build the little islands over a period of hundreds of years—mostly between the 1200s and the 1600s. Later they were abandoned by all—except for the ghosts who are said to still guard them.

Some of the human-made islands that make up Nan Madol

The **ancient** city of Nan Madol lies just off the coast of Pohnpei, a natural island that was home to a group of people known as the Saudeleurs. These islanders used log-shaped stones to build a city made up of 92 **islets**. Around these tiny islands, they built high walls to keep the ocean waves from washing the city away.

Nan Madol was the place where the families of powerful chiefs lived. It was also the place where priests lived and took care of the **tombs** in which the bodies of the chiefs were laid to rest.

Over time, the people of Nan Madol left their city. No one knows exactly why, though some believe it became too difficult to bring fresh food and water to the islands. Even today, few people visit Nan Madol because it is so hard to reach. According to those who live nearby, the visitors who do manage to reach Nan Madol are in for a shock. That's because ghosts are said to haunt and protect the **ruins** of the city that was once their home.

It is still unknown how the islanders who built Nan Madol managed to move the heavy stones they used. According to **legend**, the ancient builders used magic to get the heavy **slabs** to fly into place.

The ruins of Nan Madol

Going Downhill

Craco, Italy

The sturdy stone houses of Craco, Italy, were built high on a hill to keep people safe from enemies. Unfortunately, the buildings could not protect the people from the many disasters that would strike the city.

The abandoned
city of Craco

The huge tower that marks the highest point in Craco dates back to around 1,000 A.D. At that time, the people who lived there needed the structure to watch for invaders approaching from the surrounding countryside. Over the next 500 years, the town grew, and more buildings filled up the steep hilltop.

Although Craco was not attacked or destroyed by enemies, the town suffered disaster after disaster in the centuries that followed. In 1656, **plague** swept through. The terrible illness killed hundreds of people. During the 1800s and 1900s earthquakes struck and landslides occurred. In addition, bad weather conditions killed the crops in nearby fields. Finally, in 1963, it was decided that the town had become completely unsafe as a result of these natural disasters. All the remaining residents were moved to a nearby valley, and the town was abandoned.

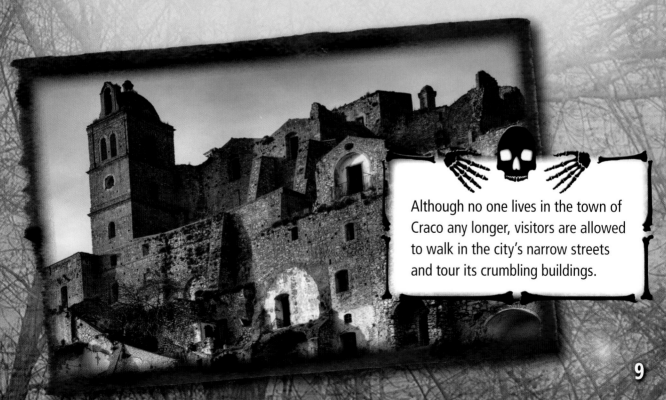

Although no one lives in the town of Craco any longer, visitors are allowed to walk in the city's narrow streets and tour its crumbling buildings.

Swallowed by the Sea

Dunwich, England

At one time, Dunwich, England, was a booming town. Thanks to its seaside location, it was an important **port** city, naval base, and fishing and shipbuilding center. Over the years, however, the same sea that had brought so much growth and success to the town also caused most of its homes, churches, businesses—and people—to disappear.

The ruins of Dunwich

By 1100, Dunwich had one of the largest populations of all the cities in England and was the capital of a region known as East Anglia. Then, in January of 1286, a giant storm hit. Huge waves washed over a large part of the town and swept it into the sea. More storms followed over the years, and so did more destruction. By the early 1900s, most of Dunwich's buildings had been lost to the restless North Sea.

Today, Dunwich is a tiny village. Only about a hundred people live there. Where there were once more than a dozen churches, there are now only the crumbling ruins of one church. Still, the town's remaining residents are sometimes reminded of the churches that once stood, since they say that church bells can sometimes be heard rising up from beneath the waves.

Waves crashing onto Dunwich beach

All Saints' Church, the last church to be lost in Dunwich, had a cemetery. One gravestone from it has been left behind. It stands about 15 feet (5 m) from the edge of a cliff that is constantly pounded by waves.

A Drowned Town Reappears

Old Adaminaby, Australia

Sometimes cities and towns are lost underwater because of floods or other forces of nature. There are also times, however, when an entire community is deliberately **submerged**. Such places then become known as "drowned towns." One of the most famous—and strangest—of these sunken towns is Old Adaminaby.

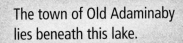

The town of Old Adaminaby lies beneath this lake.

In 1957, Australians were working on a huge engineering project. Its purpose was to capture water from melting winter snows and use it to create two large lakes. The water collected in the lakes would then be released to help farmers grow crops and to power spinning wheels called **turbines**, which help produce electricity.

To create one of the lakes, the project's engineers had to flood a town called Adaminaby. They moved some of the town's homes and buildings to nearby dry land and submerged others. At that point, the newly built settlement was named New Adaminaby, and the town at the bottom of the lake became known as Old Adaminaby.

Exactly 50 years later, in 2007, a terrible drought hit. As water in the lake that covered Old Adaminaby slowly dried up, houses, trees, trucks, and other parts of the abandoned town slowly reappeared—like ghosts that had come back to haunt the living.

When the water level is normal, trout fishing is a popular activity on the lake that flooded Old Adaminaby.

This house in Old Adaminaby reappeared during the drought in 2007.

The City of the Crystal Skull

Lubaantun, Belize

More than a thousand years ago, the Mayan people built great cities in a part of the world that is now made up of Mexico, Belize, Guatemala, El Salvador, and Honduras. In the early 1900s, an expert who studied Mayan **sites** came upon a city that was unlike any he had ever seen before. Did one young woman also find an object that has supernatural powers there?

The Maya were great builders. Within their cities were palaces, temples, and pyramids. Usually, these mighty buildings were made up of large rectangular blocks that were carved from stone and held in place with **mortar**.

Ruins at Lubaantun

In 1903, a British **archaeologist** named Thomas Gann learned from modern-day villagers about a large area of ruins in Belize. When he explored them, he was amazed at what he found. The ancient city, called Lubaantun, had within it eleven large buildings. They were different from other known Mayan buildings because they were mostly built without the use of mortar and had rounded corners.

During the 1950s, Lubaantun became known for another unusual find. An English writer named F. A. Mitchell-Hedges claimed he had a beautifully made life-size crystal skull from the ancient ruins. Both Mitchell-Hedges and his daughter, Anna, stated that Anna had found the skull in a temple when the two of them were in Lubaantun in the 1920s—even though there was no proof that Anna had ever been at the site. Later during her lifetime, Anna would also claim that the skull—which came to be known as the "Skull of Doom"—had mysterious powers, including the power to bring about a deadly **curse**.

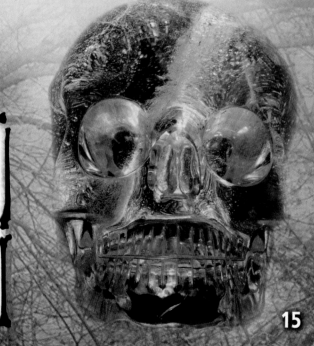

Several experts who have done scientific tests on the skull have concluded that it was made in modern times and, therefore, could not have actually come from Lubaantun. Still, some people today continue to speak and write about its Mayan origin and its supernatural qualities.

Buried in Sand

Kolmanskop, Namibia

Every day, the blazing hot sun of the Namib Desert beats down on a spooky sight. Well-built houses, some with fancy decorations, rise up from the sand—but they stand empty. Why was there once such a grand-looking city in the middle of a harsh desert? Why did its inhabitants vanish within a short time?

One day in 1908, a worker named Zacharias Lewala was shoveling sand near a railroad track that ran through part of the Namib Desert. He saw something glittering and picked it up to take a closer look. The sparkling object was a diamond.

Abandoned houses in Kolmanskop

Word of the lucky find spread quickly. By 1910, a town had sprung up to provide a home for those who flocked to the area to gather up the precious stones. The town, called Kolmanskop, included not only houses, but also a school, hospital, theater, ballroom, and ice factory. Because the company that ran the **prospecting** operation was German, the buildings were designed to look like those in a well-off German town.

By the 1920s, almost all the diamonds had been removed from the area. At that point, the people who had come to Kolmanskop because of them began to leave. By 1956, everyone had left. It wasn't long before sand carried by the desert winds covered the streets. As windows broke and doors blew open, sand also entered the houses and buildings, leaving a knee-deep layer. Now, more than 50 years later, Kolmanskop lies buried by time and the desert.

Today, visitors can tour what is left of Kolmanskop during the day. According to some who live nearby, it's lucky that the abandoned town is closed at night. Why? People claim that after darkness falls, ghosts come out to visit the places where they used to live and spend time.

Inside a home filled with sand

Built and Then Forgotten

Hashima Island, Japan

About nine miles (14 km) off the coast of Japan lies an island called Hashima. Some people call it Battleship Island, since, with its tall concrete buildings and high **seawalls**, it looks like a giant battleship floating in the dark, choppy ocean waters. Others call it Ghost Island, because it is now only a ghost of its former self.

Hashima Island

Hashima was once one of more than 500 rocky, completely **uninhabited** islands off Japan's southwestern coast. Then, in the 1890s, a large company called Mitsubishi began a **mining** project to dig out the coal that was in the seafloor around the island. At first, workers traveled from the Japanese mainland to their jobs by **ferry**. Later, however, Mitsubishi built huge blocks of apartment buildings on Hashima so that the workers could live there. By the late 1950s, there were more than 5,000 people on the tiny island—making it one of the most crowded places on Earth.

Just as the population of Hashima was reaching its peak, oil was becoming Japan's most important energy source. As a result, the demand for coal went down, and so did the amount of mining done from Hashima. Finally, in 1974, the island was shut down completely and all the people moved away. With no one left to take care of them, buildings and seawalls began crumbling. The only sounds to be heard in a place that was once as crowded as any city in the world were the crashing of the waves and the whistling of the wind.

Crumbling buildings on Hashima

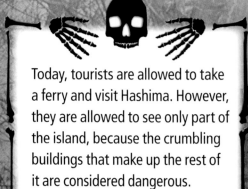

Today, tourists are allowed to take a ferry and visit Hashima. However, they are allowed to see only part of the island, because the crumbling buildings that make up the rest of it are considered dangerous.

A Nuclear Nightmare

Pripyat, Ukraine

In 1970, a brand-new city had been built in Ukraine and was ready for workers and their families to move in. Only 16 years later, however, its houses, schools, and shops were emptied of people almost overnight. The modern, up-to-date city, called Pripyat, had been the victim of a deadly disaster.

An abandoned amusement park in Pripyat

20

Pripyat was built to provide a home for workers at the Chernobyl **nuclear** power plant. Inside the plant's buildings, machines called reactors split the **atoms** of a metal called uranium. The process was used to produce heat, which, in turn, was used to produce electricity.

The kind of energy produced at Chernobyl can be extremely dangerous if the uranium gets too hot—which is exactly what happened on April 26, 1986. An explosion and fire occurred in one of the reactors, sending a cloud of poisonous smoke over Pripyat. Several people living in the city became sick right away, but residents were not told to leave until the next day. At that point, they were told to bring only a few items with them, since they could expect to be back in a few days.

Those who left, however, never returned. The fire and smoke at Chernobyl turned out to be the worst nuclear accident in history. Meanwhile, Pripyat—**contaminated** for years to come—remains frozen in time, filled with the clothes, toys, books, photographs, and other belongings that were left behind.

Many people died as a result of the accident at Chernobyl, but experts disagree about the number. Some say that there were at least 5,000 deaths due to **radiation** sickness and **cancer** caused by poisons in the air. Others think that tens of thousands of people who were in the area around the nuclear plant died as a result of the accident.

An abandoned classroom

A Ghost Town from the Future

San Zhi, Taiwan

The town of San Zhi was built to be a fancy **resort** for the rich—but it was not just another vacation spot. Its waterfront apartments looked like something out of the future. Some people even said they looked like UFOs. Unfortunately, the unusual structures were abandoned before anyone had a chance to stay in them.

Apartments at San Zhi

Work on the San Zhi apartments began in 1978. During the next two years, construction crews completed several buildings that looked like pods, or shells. Because of the odd design of its structures, people began to call the building project the "pod village."

While the work was going on, an unusually high number of accidents took place, and several workers died. As a result, the project's owners and managers stopped the building process in 1980. For the next 28 years, the pod village stood empty and still. Walls began to crumble and roofs started caving in. People living nearby began to say that the ghosts of the workers who had been killed now haunted the abandoned resort.

Finally, at the end of 2008, those in charge of the project decided to tear down the pod village. They began taking steps to replace it with a new seaside resort and water park. Will San Zhi's ghosts move on now that their dwelling place has been demolished? Or will they stay behind and take their place in the new **luxury** residences?

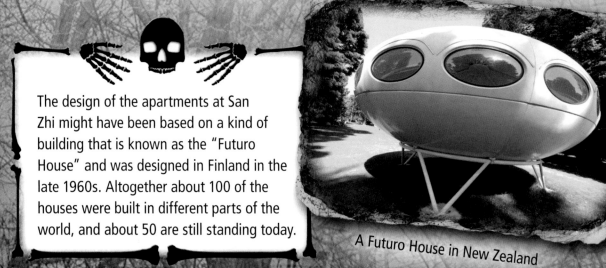

The design of the apartments at San Zhi might have been based on a kind of building that is known as the "Futuro House" and was designed in Finland in the late 1960s. Altogether about 100 of the houses were built in different parts of the world, and about 50 are still standing today.

A Futuro House in New Zealand

An Ancient Legend Comes True

Troy, Present-Day Turkey

According to one of the world's most famous legends, there was once a mighty city not far from ancient Greece. High walls wrapped all the way around the city to help defend it from enemies. They proved useless, however, against a deadly trick that was thought up by a clever leader on the enemy side.

The ancient ruins of Troy

The walled city of Troy was made famous by two ancient poets—a Greek named Homer and a Roman named Virgil. Each told about a war between the Greeks and the people of Troy, called Trojans.

For ten long years, the Greek army surrounded Troy but was unable to enter its walls. Finally, Odysseus, a Greek general, had an idea—to build a wooden horse so big that he and a group of warriors could hide inside it. The Greeks built the horse and then left it outside the city's walls. When the Trojans brought it inside, the fighters spilled out and opened the gates of the city so that more of their soldiers could enter. The Greeks then killed most of the people within and burned Troy down.

For a long time no one knew if Troy had really existed. Then, in 1870, a German archaeologist named Heinrich Schliemann began digging for the ancient city in a hill in Turkey. Before long, he had uncovered layers of ruins showing that, over time, nine different cities had stood in that spot. Today, experts agree that one was probably the real-life Troy.

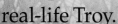

Archaeologists studying the site in Turkey think that the seventh layer from the bottom, known as Troy VII, is the walled city destroyed by the Greeks.

This model shows what the Trojan horse might have looked like.

25

Searching for a Sunken City

Atlantis—Location Unknown

Did a magnificent city filled with people who had an amazing amount of knowledge about building, farming, sailing, and many other areas exist in ancient times—long before the Egyptians, Greeks, and Romans? For more than 2,000 years, many have believed that it did, and some have even searched for it. Others, however, doubt that there ever was such a place at all.

An artist's view of what Atlantis might have looked like

Around 360 B.C., a Greek **philosopher** named Plato wrote about an island called Atlantis. In the center of the island was a beautiful city that contained a palace and many other beautiful homes, along with temples, statues, fountains, and **canals**. The people who lived there were not only great builders but also great sailors and traders who traveled all over the world.

Over the centuries, however, the Atlanteans became greedy and disrespectful. As a result, the Greek gods punished the islanders by causing earthquakes that made the island sink into the sea.

Today, long after Plato's time, people disagree about Atlantis. To many, it is simply part of a story Plato made up to teach a lesson about how people should live. Others, however—including some archaeologists and explorers—point out that Plato included a great deal of factual information about the island's location. To them, Atlantis is a real city that was lost and will someday be found.

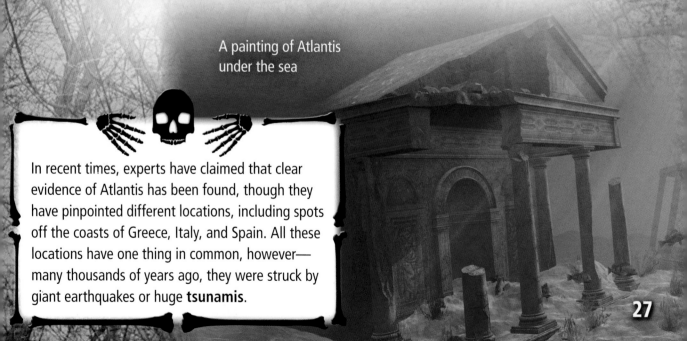

A painting of Atlantis under the sea

In recent times, experts have claimed that clear evidence of Atlantis has been found, though they have pinpointed different locations, including spots off the coasts of Greece, Italy, and Spain. All these locations have one thing in common, however— many thousands of years ago, they were struck by giant earthquakes or huge **tsunamis**.

Lost Cities

Dunwich, England
Over centuries, one building after another is lost to the sea.

Craco, Italy
A city that could slide down a steep hill is abandoned.

NORTH AMERICA

Atlantic Ocean

Lubaantun, Belize
Did pyramid builders from long ago also make a beautiful crystal skull?

SOUTH AMERICA

Atlantis
Location Unknown
Explorers continue to search for a city that may or may not be real.

Pacific Ocean

Kolmanskop, Namibia
Where diamonds once glittered, only sand remains.

Around the World

Pripyat, Ukraine
A city is poisoned by a nuclear accident.

Hashima Island, Japan
One of the world's most crowded places suddenly empties out.

ARCTIC Ocean

ASIA

EUROPE

Troy, Present-Day Turkey
A city destroyed by an ancient war is finally discovered.

Pacific Ocean

AFRICA

Indian Ocean

San Zhi, Taiwan
A resort city that seems to belong to the future is never finished.

AUSTRALIA

Nan Madol, Micronesia
Tiny islands were built for powerful chiefs— and for their tombs.

Old Adaminaby, Australia
A once-sunken city rises again.

Southern Ocean

ANTARCTICA

Glossary

abandoned (uh-BAN-duhnd) left empty

ancient (AYN-shunt) very old

archaeologist (ar-kee-OL-uh-jist) a scientist who learns about ancient times by studying things he or she digs up

atoms (AT-uhmz) tiny building blocks that make up every substance in the universe

canals (kuh-NALZ) narrow stretches of water that are dug across land

cancer (KAN-sur) a serious, often deadly disease that destroys parts of the body

contaminated (kuhn-TAM-uh-nayt-id) made polluted or unfit for use

curse (KURSS) something that brings or causes evil or misfortune

ferry (FEHR-ee) a boat that travels back and forth from one place to another

goods (GUDZ) things that are sold

industry (IN-duh-stree) a type of business

islets (EYE-luhts) tiny islands

legend (LEJ-uhnd) a story handed down from the past that may be based on fact but is not always completely true

luxury (LUHK-shuh-ree) something expensive and beautiful that makes life enjoyable and pleasant

mining (MYE-ning) the digging of deep holes or tunnels from which rock or other materials are taken

mortar (MOR-tur) a mixture of sand, limestone, water, and cement that is spread and hardened between bricks or stones to hold them together

nuclear (NOO-klee-ur) having to do with a type of energy that is produced by splitting atoms

philosopher (fuh-LOS-uh-fur) a person who thinks and writes about the meaning of life

plague (PLAYG) a disease that spreads quickly and often kills many people

port (PORT) a place where ships load and unload goods

prospecting (PROS-pekt-ing) searching the ground for gold, gems, or other valuable resources

radiation (ray-dee-AY-shuhn) a form of energy that can be very dangerous

resort (ri-ZORT) a place where people on vacation relax

ruins (ROO-inz) what is left of something that has collapsed or been destroyed

seawalls (SEE-wawlz) walls that are built to keep tides and waves from washing buildings or land into the ocean

sites (SYETS) places or locations

slabs (SLABZ) flat, thick pieces of something

spirits (SPIHR-its) supernatural creatures, such as ghosts

submerged (suhb-MURJD) covered with water

tombs (TOOMZ) graves, rooms, or buildings in which dead bodies are placed

tsunamis (tsoo-NAH-meez) giant ocean waves caused by earthquakes or volcanic eruptions

turbines (TUR-byenz) machines that are powered by wind, water, or steam moving through the blades of a wheel and making it spin

uninhabited (uhn-in-HAB-it-id) having no people living there

30

Bibliography

Burke-Gaffney, Brian. "Hashima: The Ghost Island." *Cabinet Magazine*, Summer 2002 (http://www.cabinetmagazine.org/issues/7/hashima.php).

Curran, Bob. *Lost Lands, Forgotten Realms.* Franklin Lakes, NJ: New Page Books (2007).

Lamy, Matt. *100 Strangest Mysteries.* New York: Metro Books (2007).

Rosen, Brenda. *The Atlas of Lost Cities: Legendary Cities Rediscovered.* London: Godsfield Press (2007).

Read More

Hamilton, Sue. *Lost Cities (Unsolved Mysteries).* Edina, MN: Abdo Publishing (2008).

Hook, Jason. *Lost Cities (Mysteries of the Past).* Austin, TX: Raintree (2003).

Parvis, Sarah. *Ghost Towns (Scary Places).* New York: Bearport (2008).

Stern, Steven L. *Wretched Ruins (Scary Places).* New York: Bearport (2010).

Learn More Online

To learn more about lost cities, visit
www.bearportpublishing.com/ScaryPlaces

Index

About the Author

Natalie Lunis has written many nonfiction books for children. She lives in New York's lower Hudson River Valley, just north of New York City.